Get It Together

Five Simple Strategies for Becoming Reliable, Saving Time, and Making Fewer Mistakes

By Matthew Canning

influxa

Get It Together ©2015 Matthew Canning

Published by the Influxa Media Group

Edited by Erin Thorp

Cover art and design by IredHands

ISBN 978-0692425695

First Edition: April 2015 | Second Edition: March 2018

In 2009, Philadelphia community organizer Chris Bartlett gave a presentation in which he suggested that everyone should select several "mentors and protégés." For example, you may have a mentor from whom you seek ethical or professional guidance. You may have a protégé that gets the same benefits from you.

However, Bartlett uniquely suggests that it should all be done in secret. Your mentors should never explicitly know that you seek to emulate them, and your protégés should never feel as though you've actively taken them under your wing. This eliminates for everyone involved the pressures and expectations that might result from formalizing such relationships.

This book is dedicated to my secret mentors and protégés.

Contents

Introduction

We all know someone who constantly misses appointments, forgets things, shows up late, and produces sub-par work. Despite intelligence and good intentions, their life is a constant struggle. Imagine this individual. How do you feel about them?

We also know someone else who's always on time, overly prepared, and calm. Everything they produce is well thought-out and polished. Despite a busy life and demanding responsibilities, their life seems easy. Imagine this person too. How do they do it?

Where do you fall?

Most of us are somewhere in between, but you can learn simple strategies that make a huge difference. Just five small adjustments (and a little practice) can make you more focused, punctual, and responsible, setting you dramatically apart from the bumbling, chronically distracted masses.

Get It Together takes a systems engineering approach to reducing risk and oversight, presented in practical ways you can easily integrate into your daily life. You'll learn how to improve the quality of everything you do. You'll eliminate the most common problems that affect the events and actions that collectively make up the narrative of your life.

Strategy 1: Check In

Checking In is a tool for increasing awareness that consists of habitually asking a series of questions before and after every single thing you do. That's right: *every single thing*. The practice isn't restricted to specific tasks, professional applications, or complex actions; it's constant and context-agnostic. Over the course of this lesson, you'll drive yourself to the brink of insanity by overanalyzing every action and intention until it becomes natural and automatic.

This may seem daunting and unnecessary, but is it really?

I've seen people get off the subway without their grocery bags. I've seen a man leave an expensive dry-cleaned suit in a public park. I've seen a woman ask a convenience store clerk if she "left keys on the counter a few hours ago." I've seen people arrive at the Canadian border without identification. Back in college, I lost an entire trombone. Our personal system—or complete lack thereof—for preventing such forgetfulness is clearly flawed. We're worse off than we care to admit.

Checking In to the rescue.

Checking In means running through a mental list when transitioning between settings. A loose form of this strategy is commonly implemented when a special situation arises—whenever you think there's a risk that something might be forgotten. Standing at your front door about to leave home for a long weekend trip, you would probably stop and say, "Okay. Toiletries, phone charger, clothes, medicine, wallet..."

Unfortunately, when it comes to more common situations, the risk of oversight isn't always apparent until it's too late. You most likely didn't run through a mental **Check-In** when you last sat down at your computer or left your bedroom. Most people assume they're unlikely to forget things under normal circumstances, and so feel as though regular, habitual **Check-Ins** would be a waste of time and mental energy. The fact is, almost everyone forgets things on a regular basis; it's simply so commonplace that society as a whole is typically understanding of forgetfulness and oversight.

Constantly and habitually **Checking In** can help you to maintain focus in the face of constant distractions. Consciously or not, people who "have it together" may be performing a **Check-In**-like action without thinking, and others simply may not have developed the skill naturally. It's certainly not taught in school, so we are left to develop it on our own.

The first thing to learn is how and when to **Check In,** and then how to transition **Checking In** from an intrusive conscious practice to a subconscious one that requires no special dedication of time or energy— a natural part of your thinking process.

How to Check In

Checking In may seem like a common sense task, and you probably think you already know how to do it. However, most undisciplined **Check-Ins** go something like, "Okay, what did I forget? Is this everything I need? Hmmmm." Rather than trying to "jog" memories with no clear direction, here you'll learn to ask specific **Action Questions**. Most people don't project their mind into the immediate future; they just "think really hard" in the present with no plan. Thinking hard doesn't work. Thinking *strategically* does.

Your new process will involve running through a predefined **Check-In** *before leaving a setting or situation* (a **"Departure" Check-In**), and *upon arriving at a new setting or situation* (an **"Arrival" Check-In**). It's that simple.

The Departure Check-In

Train yourself to habitually ask the following **Action Questions** *before leaving a setting or situation*:

1. Did I accomplish the task(s) I planned to accomplish?
2. Is anything out of the ordinary that will require special attention?
3. Will I need anything else from this location in the immediate future (even considering unlikely possibilities)?

How many times have you driven home and walked into your house only to realize that you forgot to bring something with you from the car? Perhaps you left your wallet in the glove box or a sweaty t-shirt from the gym in the back seat. Things like this happen all the time, and you probably just accept them as part of life. Getting out of a car isn't a special event, so you're not conditioned to **Check In** when it happens.

Consider this scenario again, but this time with a **Departure Check-In**. As you are about to get out of the car, you ask **Action Question** 1 from the above list: *Did I accomplish the task(s) I planned to accomplish?* This is an open-ended question that can bring to mind many different (and perfectly valid) interpretations. *Why was I out and about? Where did I plan to go, and did I get there? What did I plan to do, and did I do it?* This could tip you off if you forgot to run an errand or get fuel while you were out. This question should cause you to project your consciousness into the immediate past, assess the trip you took and your intentions for the trip, and decide whether or not you accomplished the trip's primary or peripheral goals.

Action Question 2: *Is anything out of the ordinary that will require special attention?* Moving on from the past, **Action Question** 2 brings your awareness to the present and your physical setting. Where are you? Is everything the way it should be? This should prompt you to quickly scan the interior of the vehicle and the surrounding area. "Out of the ordinary" can be interpreted many ways, and can cause you to notice both immediate situational cues (such as something sitting on your dashboard or passenger seat that needs to be taken into the house) and "big picture" information (like your car's odometer reaching mileage that requires a routine tune-up).

Action Question 3: *Will I need anything else from this location in the immediate future (even considering unlikely possibilities)?* This question transports your thoughts into the future. This might remind you of some paperwork in your glove box that needs to be taken inside. Or perhaps you're being picked up by a friend later in the day, and will need to take your sunglasses with you; this question should remind you to bring them in from the car. The parenthetical text, "*even considering unlikely possibilities*" forces you to consider not only your *planned* path for the next few hours, but also possible alternatives. If your spouse or roommate comes home earlier than expected, will you have to move your car? What if your friend got sick and couldn't pick you up after all?

You may be thinking that this practice is invasive, distracting, and obsessive, and you'd be correct. However, once **Checking In** becomes an ingrained habit, these questions won't need to be consciously asked; you'll simply be aware of the need to answer them. Many people who seem to naturally "have it together" already engage in some form of this practice subconsciously; they most likely learned to do so at an early age. While catching up, the rest of us will have to engage in this practice consciously; for now, that may seem strange and annoying.

In certain cases, some of these **Action Questions** may seem as though they don't apply. If you just woke up and rolled out of bed, *"Did I accomplish the task(s) I came here to accomplish?"* doesn't seem like a logical question to ask. "I came here to sleep. I slept. Case closed." But is it really that cut-and-dry? I can't tell you how many times I have gotten up and walked downstairs only to hear the alarm clock I forgot to turn off begin to buzz again from my bedroom. **Action Question** 2 (*"Is there anything out of the ordinary that will require special attention?"*) may remind you that the bed sheets need washing, and so you should strip them and take them downstairs to the laundry room to save yourself a trip later. It may cause you to realize that your spouse left something next to the bed he or she will need. **Action Question** 3 (*"Will I need anything else from this location in the immediate future?"*) might prompt you to unplug your cell phone and take it with you, or to get some clothes together. Projecting your consciousness into the immediate future could also trigger other reminders; for instance, it may remind you to arrive at work earlier than usual to prepare for a meeting.

Performing regular **Check-Ins** gets you in the habit of taking quick mental snapshots of your position in both time and space. It keeps you acutely aware of your situation throughout the day, including your immediate past and future. The value of this practice is simple and profound: if you actually perform a **Departure Check-In** at every opportunity, you'll be drastically more prepared and reduce instances of forgetfulness and oversight. This reduces the amount of negativity in life. Fewer excuses. Fewer apologies. Less regret. The more you practice **Departure Check-Ins** (even when they seem pointless), the more they'll become routine and natural, and the less invasive and obsessive they'll seem. They'll eventually require no conscious thought whatsoever.

The Arrival Check-In

Check-Ins should also be performed *upon arriving at a new setting or situation*. This time, ask the following **Action Questions**:

1. Did I accomplish everything I was supposed to accomplish at my last location?
2. Did I forget anything from my last location that I need now, or may need in the immediate future (even considering unlikely possibilities)?
3. What tasks have I come here to accomplish?
4. Is anything out of the ordinary that will require special attention?

These **Action Questions** are split into two parts. The first two questions are a backup for the last **Departure Check-In**, and the next two relate to the new setting.

After the "getting out of the car" scenario, imagine stepping into your house, and—because it's a new setting—running through your **Arrival Check-In**. The first two questions cover anything that may have been missed during the **Departure Check-In** back in the car. This is a concept called **Redundancy**: ensuring that you're doing an adequate job of **Checking In** by exposing each transition (the trip from one location to the next) to two independent reviews.

Let's say you didn't run a comprehensive **Departure Check-In** when exiting your car. You would then find yourself in your house, performing your **Arrival Check-In**. You ask the first two questions *("Did I accomplish everything I was supposed to accomplish in the car?"* and *"Did I forget anything from the car that I need now, or may need in the immediate future?"*). These questions cause you to review and catch anything you may have missed in failing to go through a thorough **Departure Check-In**.

Once you're finished reinforcing your **Departure Check-In** with the first two **Arrival Check-In Action Questions**, you can forget about the past and settle your consciousness into the present setting.

The final two **Action Questions** reset your focus and alert you to any current or future circumstances that may require alterations to your plan. Consider **Action Question** 3: *"What tasks have I come here to accomplish?"* Answering this lets you take a quick inventory of both immediate and longer-term goals in your new location. In this example, the question is asking, "Why did I come home?" You may have come home for the night to eat dinner, pay some bills, spend time with your family, and go to bed; or, you might only be at home briefly to pick something or someone up. Perhaps this question is a reminder of something specific you need to do before other people get home, or to pack your lunch for the next day. If you approach it with an open mind, this question can provide a good deal of value.

When you're reasonably sure you've remembered all the tasks you need to accomplish in this new setting, move on to **Action Question** 4: "*Is there anything out of the ordinary that will require special attention?*" Looking around, you may realize something small (the trash needs to go out). This question can also serve as a way to minimize risk: a scan of the kitchen before leaving for work in the morning could reveal an open window, a loose chair leg, a plug hanging halfway out of an outlet, or a coffee pot left on. How many times have you been suddenly struck with the fear that you left the stove on? Knowing that you performed a **Check-In** can ease this anxiety. This **Action Question** will help get you in the practice of quickly scanning your surroundings, a habit that can be surprisingly insightful. Continued practice will heighten your overall awareness of surroundings and situations. It could even save your life; **Situational Awareness** is a concept taught at all levels of emergency response and law enforcement that involves developing a heightened awareness of your surroundings in order to identify potential threats.

By **Checking In** properly, you should catch a high percentage of the little things you would otherwise miss or forget, helping you avoid forgetfulness and oversight despite the constant onslaught of distractions that life presents.

Imagine this: you're at your desk working and decide to print something. You walk towards the printer, but are stopped by a coworker, Ray.

After a deep, cleansing breath, you prepare for the impending vortex of small-talk. "Oh, really, your daughter is in her high school performance of Titanic: The Musical? Cool. I'm sorry, I really don't have the time to commit to your softball league, but I appreciate the invitation. No, I don't quite remember where I got the tie. Yeah, I like paisley too. Yes, the Packers are definitely looking strong this year." You survive the conversation and realize you need to use the restroom. Since you're already standing, you might as well head over there. Once back at your desk, Tim comes by (not "nice Tim," but "creepy Tim," who never seems to blink). "Is this yours?" he asks, holding the item you printed out.

Now creepy Tim is talking to you about his affinity for the smell of gasoline, and he's going on for a long, long time. You can feel your life slipping through your fingers.

How could this tragedy have been avoided?

You guessed it: by habitually **Checking In**. You lost track of the original task. The end of your conversation with Ray (1), the moment before you left the bathroom (2), and the moment you arrived back at your desk (3) were all opportunities to run through the appropriate **Check-In Action Questions**. Doing so even *once* would have reminded you to go retrieve the item from the printer and saved you from having to interact with creepy Tim.

This example was cartoonish, but it illustrates that asking yourself these simple **Action Questions** will, in most cases, transport your consciousness back to the **Moment of Intention**, no matter how many steps (or distractions) ago it may have been.

Walk yourself through your activities over the last day or so. Did you forget something or forget to do something? Could **Checking In** have prevented oversight, kept you on track, or helped to improve your efficiency?

If you can't think of something, you're not thinking hard enough.

The Road to Automatic Check-Ins

These **Action Questions** will need to be asked consciously at first; however—as mentioned earlier—if you allow adequate time to practice **Checking In**, it will eventually become instant and automatic. You'll simply become aware of the need to answer the appropriate **Action Questions** without asking them. Done in a flash, the questions will unobtrusively make their way in and out of your mind.

Please don't interpret my promotion of productivity habits like **Checking In** as a condemnation of technological assistance. It's fine to use tools— such as smartphone calendars and to-do-lists—to stay on track in the broader sense, but it's wise to supplement external assistance with an arsenal of well-formed personal habits that benefit you moment-by-moment. **Checking In** is just one of these habits. **Task Serialization** and **Task Batching** are two others, which you'll learn about next.

Before moving on, spend two or three days obsessively **Checking In**. By the end, you should be:

1. Able to repeat the **Checking In Action Questions** (both **Arrival** and **Departure**) by heart, quickly and easily.
2. On the road to becoming aware of the questions without actively asking them.

I've often been asked if you should ask these **Action Questions** when you're only in a location for a few moments; if you're simply going to the hall closet to grab a flashlight, do you really need to perform both an **Arrival** and **Departure Check-In?** For now, while practicing and getting used to the idea, stop and run through the questions in *every* situation. No exceptions. Once they become automatic and you see how beneficial they can be, you'll most likely agree that their value far outweighs the work involved, even when you find yourself in a location only briefly.

Take as much time as you need to ingrain this. Everyone forms habits at different rates and this is an important skill that can skyrocket your productivity and reliability.

Quick Review

1. **Checking In** is the act of habitually asking a series of formal **Action Questions** upon leaving or arriving at a setting. Asked consciously at first, the questions eventually become so ingrained in your mind that they are effortless and instant.
2. The three **Departure Check-In Action Questions** to be asked before leaving a setting/situation are: (1) *Did I accomplish the task(s) I planned to accomplish?* (2) *Is anything out of the ordinary that will require special attention?* and (3) *Will I need anything else from this location in the immediate future (even considering unlikely possibilities)?*

3. The four **Arrival Check-In Action Questions** to be asked when you first arrive in a new setting/situation are: (1) *Did I accomplish everything I was supposed to accomplish at my last location?* (2) *Did I forget anything from my last location that I need now, or may need in the immediate future (even considering unlikely possibilities)?* (3) *What tasks have I come here to accomplish?* and (4) *Is anything out of the ordinary that will require special attention?*

Strategy 2: Serialize

I've always been naturally scatter-brained, and as a result, I regularly left the house without something I needed. As a teen, I developed the habit of placing objects I knew I'd need in the morning (like concert tickets, a paycheck to deposit, etc.) inside my sneakers the night before. Obviously, I wasn't leaving the house barefoot, and so I'd be sure to find the objects. Since I usually put my sneakers on right before leaving the house, this simple practice minimized my chances of forgetting the items.

How to Serialize Tasks

The basic premise of this method has merit that can be extended. It's difficult to overlook a task that is reliant upon the completion of another, unavoidable task. This is called **Serializing**: ordering tasks such that you essentially *have* to perform one in order to perform the other. In the sneakers example, I was forced to remove the object(s) from the shoe (task 1) in order to place it on my foot (task 2).

In a **Serial Relationship**, you need a **Blocker** and one or more **Dependents**. The **Blocker** is the necessary step that's interrupted—here, putting sneakers on—and the **Dependents** are the steps that need to be remembered—here, becoming aware of the objects in the sneaker. **Serializing** comes down to attaching **Dependents** to **Blockers**.

Here are some other practical examples of **Dependents** and **Blockers**:

- An unpaid bill sitting atop your computer's keyboard or tablet. You'll probably need to use your computer or tablet in the near future, and can't do so without becoming aware of the bill. Additionally, the visible clutter is usually an incentive to act upon the **Dependent** action (the payment of the bill) in a timely manner. In this example, the **Blocker** is using your keyboard or tablet; the ability to do so is blocked by the physical presence of the bill.

- A gift leaning against the inside of your front door. Imagine you're going to a birthday party. One way to ensure you don't forget a gift or card (the **Dependent**) is by placing it in a location that renders you unable to leave the house (the **Blocker**) without first becoming aware of it.

Other examples include placing things atop your cell phone or toothbrush, in the top of your underwear drawer, or on top of your car keys or bus pass. Take a moment right now and think of an instance when this concept could have been implemented in your own life over the past week. Even if you didn't forget any objects or tasks that you can think of, consider how you could have used a **Serial Relationship** to further ensure you'd have remembered something.

Task Serialization is a supplement to **Checking In**—not an alternative. In theory, properly **Checking In** should help prevent many of these oversights and forgotten tasks; however, it's always good to exercise as much **Redundancy** as possible (within reason).

Imagine you promised to loan a book to a coworker. In order to remember to bring it to work the next day, most people would make a note on a piece or paper or in their phone calendar. You can certainly continue to do so, but personal habits can ensure you follow through (if you end up leaving home in a rush, for instance, you may forget to check the paper or calendar). Correctly **Checking In** would tip you off to (1) take it with you when you leave for work, (2) remove it from your car or bag when you get there, and (3) give it to her when you see her in the office. **Serializing**, or connecting the book with a **Blocker**—such as setting it atop your car keys or bus pass at home—helps *ensure* you won't forget it. It works side-by-side with **Checking In** to maximize effectiveness.

You're Not Immune to Oversight

Initially, most people think this practice is extreme because they underestimate their level of oversight.

I have a friend who, strangely, kept losing hats. He almost always wears hats, and has a habit of taking them off before eating. As a result, he has donated upwards of twenty hats to the diners and restaurants of Pennsylvania, New Jersey, and New York over the last few decades. Upon my advice, he began **Serializing** the hat by placing it (as the **Dependent**) in the way of something that he would have to take with him when the meal was over (the **Blocker**).

His solutions have evolved over the years. He first began sitting his hats atop his jacket, but he would often knock the hat onto the floor without noticing. Also, he doesn't wear a jacket in the summer, so that didn't work. For a while, he placed his hat on top of his girlfriend's purse— when she would pick up her purse before leaving, she (being more naturally observant than he) would see the hat and hand it to him. However, this solution wasn't perfect either. He finally began placing his hat next to him with his car keys inside. If he forgot the hat or if it fell off the seat, he wouldn't be able to leave the parking lot without realizing and going back.

Everyone I know seems to consistently forget something or other: leaving their doors unlocked, or forgetting to charge their cell phones, or often finding themselves at the grocery store without a list. **Checking In** would help mitigate such oversight, but even if **Checking In** fails, you can develop creative solutions to these problems through **Serialization**.

Just Begin

The best way to get used to **Task Serialization** is just to begin implementing the concept as often as possible. Get creative, don't worry about appearing strange, and even **Serialize** tasks or items you don't think you're likely to forget; no one truly thinks that they'll forget to do something until it's too late (as the saying goes, hindsight is 20/20). While continuing to **Check In**, begin **Serializing** your life. Get in the habit of placing objects or reminders atop **Blockers**. Overdo it for a while, and it will become more natural with time. Don't move on until you feel completely comfortable with **Task Serialization**.

Serialization isn't just for individuals; it also works for tasks that involve two or more people. If I need to remind my wife to take something with her in the morning, or if I want to leave her a note that I'm sure she'll see, I place the object or note directly in the way of something that I know she'll need, such as the coffee maker or interior handle of our front door. I've left things in her shoes that I worried she'd forget, and she's done the same for me.

It's not crazy if it works.

The two strategies you've learned so far are examples of how structured and well-executed processes can reduce human error. You're about to learn about **Task Batching**, a third example of the same idea.

Quick Review

Task Serialization is the act of attaching an easily forgotten task or item (called a **Dependent**) to a necessary task or item (called a **Blocker**), to ensure that the former is brought to your attention.

Strategy 3: Batch

> *"Obviously, the highest type of efficiency is that which can utilize existing material to the best advantage."*
>
> —*Jawaharlal Nehru, Prime Minister of India*

In the last section, *Serialize*, there was an example involving an unpaid bill placed atop a computer keyboard or tablet to ensure it would be noticed and addressed. You may ask, "Why let it get to that point? Why not just pay the bill when you first open it?" The answer may surprise you: performing every task at the earliest possible moment will waste a good deal of time over the long run. This brings us to the next strategy, **Task Batching**.

Task Batching involves performing several related tasks together; organizing tasks so as to minimize the total time, resources, or risk required to perform them. Like **Task Serialization**, **Task Batching** also diminishes the chances of forgetting a given task through its connection to other related tasks.

The Goal: Minimizing Peripheral Workload

Imagine you have to perform the following set of tasks, which will take a total of thirty minutes if you don't **Batch** them:

1. Drive to the supermarket (5 minutes)
2. Find and purchase eggs (5 minutes, including checkout)
3. Drive home (5 minutes)
4. Drive to the supermarket (5 minutes)
5. Find and purchase bread (5 minutes, including checkout)
6. Drive home (5 minutes)

If the tasks are **Batched**, you'll achieve the same results in seventeen minutes:

1. Drive to the supermarket (5 minutes)
2. Find and purchase eggs and bread (7 minutes, including checkout)
3. Drive home (5 minutes)

It's of course common sense to do the latter. You wouldn't drive to drive to and from the supermarket *twice* to purchase *two* items. Not only does this reduce the time spent accomplishing your goals, but it also reduces risk; for instance, less time driving reduces the chances of being involved in a car accident.

Most multi-step tasks are composed of two types of work: a **Primary Workload** and a **Peripheral Workload**. The **Primary Workload** is the main purpose of the task—in this case, purchasing eggs and bread. The **Peripheral Workload** is work you need to do in order to complete the **Primary Workload,** but otherwise wouldn't do—you wouldn't drive to the store and back if you didn't need to buy anything. To reframe the above scenario in these terms, you were able to reduce a thirty-minute trip to seventeen because your **Peripheral Workload** doesn't have to increase 100% for each 100% increase in the **Primary Workload**. Since every new item on the shopping list doesn't necessitate another trip to the store, the acts of purchasing these items can be **Batched**.

This is an admittedly exhaustive dissection of a simple concept, but being able to think this way will be useful when **Batching** more complex groups of tasks. Let's go back to the bill-paying example and compare the efficiency of immediately paying bills as they come in versus paying all bills at once.

For the sake of this example, imagine that online bill pay doesn't exist and you have to pay the old-fashioned way: a bill arrives in the mail, you review it, and mail a check back to the issuing party. Assume that for each bill, you need to locate a letter opener, open the envelope, review the charges, get out the checkbook, write a check, record the payment into an account register, locate a stamp, place the stamp on the envelope, and then put the stamps, checks, and register away. You then need to go out to the mailbox to mail the bill. After doing this for several bills, patterns begin to emerge; it quickly becomes apparent that aside from reviewing the individual bills and filling out the checks, this process is almost entirely composed of **Peripheral Workload** and would clearly benefit from **Task Batching**. Addressing multiple bills all at once on a regular schedule saves time by eliminating many repetitive instances of the same **Peripheral Workload**.

Do you wash every dish individually after it's used? Do you wash your hair, step out of the shower, dry off, and get back in to wash your face and body? Do you go holiday shopping for each individual on your list in separate trips? Of course not. But not all **Task Batching** opportunities are this obvious, and being conscious of the basic principles can make you aware of inefficiencies in your habits. Much like **Checking In**, most of us **Task Batch** effectively in specific cases, but fail to take advantage of the practice when it comes to most common actions we perform.

How to Task Batch

When you have several tasks to perform, ask the **Action Question**, *Could these tasks be arranged in an order that would minimize **Peripheral Workload**?*

It's that simple. This **Action Question** can be applied to a few seemingly unrelated tasks grouped together in a short period of time, or a few related tasks spread over a longer period. An example of the former could be:

- Pick Jason up from soccer practice
- Fuel up the car
- Buy cat food
- Pick up a gift card for Dave's birthday
- Drop off shirt at the tailor's
- Go to the gym

These things can clearly be **Batched**, since they're all errands that require you to leave home. Mathematically, there are 720[1] possible ways to order the above six tasks, but you can improve efficiency by placing them in an optimal order based on proximity (in the example, imagine the gym and tailor are close to one another), timing (*Pick Jason up from soccer practice* implies a specific time), or an array of other factors.

How about related tasks spread over a longer period? When my wife and I were first dating, every Sunday she would prepare and package five lunches for work that week. During this weekly session, she would gather the ingredients, make sandwiches, wrap them in foil, pack snacks, and put the ingredients away. This saved on cleanup, time spent making the food, and the stress of packing lunches while racing against the clock each morning.

Why do the same things every day, repeating and maximizing **Peripheral Workload**, when you can **Batch** and reduce it? Think of some things you've done over the past week that could have benefitted from some well-thought-out **Batching**.

Task Batching as an Extension of Checking In

Task Batching is closely related to **Checking In**. You could say that they look out for each other.

---

[1] Whenever you have an array of options and you'd like to know how many possible arrangements there are for them, take the number of options (here, it's 6) and multiply this number by *one number less* (5), then by *one number less* (4), and so on, until you reach 1. In this example, $6 \times 5 \times 4 \times 3 \times 2 \times 1 = 720$. The formal mathematical term for this is "factorial" (one would say, "6 factorial is 720").

Consider this scenario: After taking a shower, you head to the closet to pick out your clothes. Before leaving the closet, you should naturally and quickly ask yourself the **Arrival Check-In Action Questions**. The questions may help you recall that you need a fresh towel, since the one you've been using was thrown into the laundry. The **Check-In** saved you from having to go into your closet twice, thus **Batching** the tasks of picking out clothes and getting a towel. **Batching** is essentially the point of the **Checking In Action Question**, *Will I need anything else from this location in the immediate future (even considering unlikely possibilities)?* This demonstrates how the five strategies taught in *Get It Together* work together to create a broader mentality shift.

A Warning: Don't Use Task Batching as a Crutch

Once you get used to **Task Batching**, it's easy to become drunk with **Batching** power and use this noble practice as an excuse for laziness.

Imagine there's a plant on your porch that needs to be brought into the basement for the winter. You make a note of it, but think, "Why make a special trip outside? It's cold and I'll have to put shoes on. I'll just bring it in tonight when I get home from work." This is acceptable **Task Batching**, since (1) it's not urgent for the plant to come inside that very second, and (2) it's certain you'll be entering the house again soon.

Now imagine you eventually bring the plant into the house, put it at the top of the basement steps, and leave it there, assuming you'll need to go down to the basement for something else in the near future. "Why go down to the basement twice?" you argue. However, this would be an incorrect use of **Task Batching**. In this case, you should just take the plant down to the basement when you first bring it into the house.

The distinction here is that while you know for certain you'll be entering your home several times in the near future, there is no reason you know of that will force you to go down into the basement anytime soon. You would be **Batching** the necessary task (taking the plant down to the basement) with an *(as-of-now) fictitious, theoretical task*. This type **Task Batching** misuse can result in things being left around your home in strange places, waiting for an excuse to be dealt with.

You could theoretically **Task Batch** to the extreme, getting to the point where you only leave your house once a week, but that's not the point. **Task Batching** shouldn't interfere with the intrinsic rhythm of your life; rather, it should enhance that rhythm by helping you to live more efficiently. Use your head, be practical, and be careful not to use **Task Batching** as an excuse. Before **Task Batching**, ask yourself if you're truly being efficient or lazy, and always follow this one rule: *never **Batch** a necessary task with an undefined future task.*

Big Batching Day

Everyone has tasks that generally recur on a monthly basis (or somewhat close to monthly basis). On the first of every month, I change my contact lenses, perform safety checks (smoke alarms, car tire pressure, etc.), organize my physical workspace, reconcile my bank records online, tidy my car, organize any files that ended up on my computer's desktop, and so on. This monthly event is called my **Big Batching Day**.

You'd be surprised how many things fit neatly into a once-monthly routine with a little stretching (my contacts should actually be changed every three weeks) or compression (my workspace usually takes more than a month to become a true mess). **Batching** things in this manner lets you recognize patterns, group like events based on where they need to be performed and what tools you need to use, and otherwise minimize **Peripheral Workload**. Additionally, a plan stops these tasks from weighing on your mind and conscience. A messy desk with no cleaning deadline constantly reminds you of your inaction, whereas knowing you will clean it on a set date lets you focus on other things guilt-free.

To use this simple time management principle, schedule a repeating monthly event in your phone's calendar or other organizational tool of your choice and include a list of all tasks you need to perform on your **Big Batching Day**. It doesn't have to be the first of the month, but that seems to makes sense for most people. Identify some tasks that you need to perform on a regular basis and determine what can be **Batched** together into a single day.

Quick Review

Task Batching involves performing several related tasks together; organizing tasks so as to minimize the total time, resources, or risk required to perform them.

Strategy 4: Front-Load

Task Front-Loading is the natural enemy of **Task Batching**. Whereas **Task Batching** means putting tasks off to maximize efficiency, **Task Front-Loading** means getting tasks out of the way as soon as possible.

After an explanation of **Task Front-Loading**, you'll learn how to reconcile these two conflicting practices.

A Simple Slogan

Task Front-Loading can be summed up with a single phrase: "Do a favor for 'future-you.'" This means that if you have the choice of performing an unpleasant task now or in the future, you should "suck it up" and do it now. It's not fun, but becomes a habit fairly easily. It reduces anticipatory dread and goes a long way toward improving peoples' perception of your character; it decreases the impression that you're lazy or prone to procrastination. Getting unpleasant tasks done without delay or complaint is a trait associated with maturity and willpower.

Consider this scenario: It's late on a Saturday night and you're in your living room, unwinding. Suddenly, thanks to your **Checking In** habits, you remember that the recycling has to go out to the curb before eight o'clock the next morning (to be fair, you should have realized this earlier if you were **Checking In** properly). You don't have work the next day, and though you'd probably wake up before eight anyway, you have no other reason to leave the house. You may think to yourself, "Oh, I'll just do it tomorrow morning." **Task Front-Loading** ("doing a favor for 'future you'") tells you to get it over with. Yes, it's unpleasant, but it won't be any more pleasant tomorrow, and you're only putting off misery temporarily. It would weigh on your mind—however subtly—until then.

On top of making "future you" happier, taking the recycling out tonight instead of tomorrow morning reduces the risk of potential problems. If the pickup happens earlier than normal, you may miss it. Even after **Checking In**, you may forget to take the recycling out in the morning. You may oversleep. There may be an unexpected emergency that prevents you from taking it out. Taking care of it now prevents these possibilities.

When In Doubt, Task Batch

When considering **Task Front-Loading**, remember that **Task Batching** trumps **Task Front-Loading**. It's a balancing act, but it's not so bad once you get used to keeping both concepts in mind.

Imagine again that you're sitting at home on a Saturday night. This time, instead of having to take the recycling out, you need to fuel up your car. It's not dangerously low on fuel, but it needs to be done before a lengthy drive on Monday. **Task Front-Loading** ("doing a favor for future-you") tells you to get off your butt and go get the fuel. You can't know for certain what the next day will hold. It may rain, you may become busy with an unforeseen issue, etc. This all sounds like a great argument for **Task Front-Loading**.

However, imagine one of your many habitual daily **Check-Ins** reveals that you also need to pick something up from a friend before you leave for the aforementioned trip. Since it's too late at night to bother your friend, **Front-Loading** the fuel task would mean going out twice (once tonight to the gas station and again tomorrow to your friend's house), and so you decide to **Batch** the tasks into one trip tomorrow.

You saw how **Task Batching** trumps **Task Front-Loading**, as the **Batching** choice was made based on a *necessary and definite* future task (picking the item up from your friend). Without this (or another task that requires you to leave the house), there'd be no reason to **Batch**, and you should do "future you" a favor.

A Simple Change That Brings a Lot of Positivity

Comedian Steven Wright once said, "Hard work pays off in the future, but laziness pays off now." He's right—laziness does pay off now, and it takes maturity and discipline to understand the benefit of temporary sacrifice in the present for future convenience or long-term gain. Adopting this mindset creates a contagious, noticeable attitude shift that makes a positive impression everyone you meet.

While continuing to practice active **Check-Ins**, **Task Serialization**, and **Task Batching**, spend one week focusing on **Task Front-Loading**. Go out of your way to completely stop procrastinating. No exceptions for one week. You'll see a reduction in interpersonal tension and internal stress associated with looming responsibility. Embrace the attitude selflessly and powerfully. Overdo it. **Task Front-Loading**, approached with an air of enthusiasm, is a powerful habit. We're a society of habitual procrastinators. How many people purchase a card on the way to a wedding, pack for a trip five minutes before leaving, or drive around for days with a "low fuel" light staring them in the face? Schools are full of students finishing reports mere minutes before the deadline. All this stress can be avoided with a change in mentality.

The choice to quit procrastination cold turkey can be one of the best decisions you ever make. Kick the habit. "Future-you" will thank you.

Quick Review

Task Front-Loading formalizes the decision to act immediately upon unpleasant tasks and prevents procrastination. Opt out of **Task Front-Loading** only when the task(s) in question would benefit from **Task Batching**.

Strategy 5: Engage

A friend of mine was diagnosed with Attention Deficit Hyperactivity Disorder after struggling with symptoms for decades. He described his affliction as feeling like everything he knew and needed to access was written on sheets of paper that were circling him like a tornado. He tried to grab at thoughts but they often evaded him. After taking his first dose of medication, he felt as though the wind stopped for the first time. All the papers fell to the ground and he could suddenly organize them at will.

Whether or not you have ADHD, I suspect you can relate to some extent. It's a common experience to sometimes feel as though your responsibilities and anxieties are swirling around you, competing for your attention. In this fast paced, hyper-connected world, the ability to dedicate yourself to an individual task can seem like a luxury.

The term "mindfulness" can mean many different things. Mindfulness is one of Buddhism's seven factors of enlightenment and a tenet in many forms of yoga. Most definitions include the idea of "being in the moment," resisting the urge to think about your duties or immediate future, and resisting the urge to dwell on frustrations. Many use mindfulness and the meditation or breathing practices that often accompany it to alleviate anxiety, stress, and fatigue. In a 2006 paper entitled *Mindfulness: A Proposed Operational Definition (Clinical Psychology: Science & Practice)*, it was suggested that mindfulness "involves the self-regulation of attention so that it is maintained on immediate experience, thereby allowing for increased recognition of mental events in the present moment."

In other words, mindfulness is the practice of focusing on "the now" and what you're doing. Have you ever seen a Zen priest combing sand? Those large sandboxes, such as the famous one at the temple Ryoan-ji in Kyoto, Japan, are called Karesansui ("dry Zen gardens") and are a great example of mindfulness exercise. Zen priests rake the sand to create lines and patterns as close to perfect as possible. The point is not the end result, but the concentration and discipline involved—the practice of giving oneself wholly to the present task. Adapted, structured versions of these principles have been used with some success in western psychology to treat conditions like Obsessive Compulsive Disorder or anxiety.

Here, we'll discuss a more practical variation of mindfulness that you can integrate into daily life. Mindfulness may help you with stress, but it's included here for a different reason: it has the convenient side-effect of improving the safety, efficiency, and quality of whatever you do.

Put simply: To engage fully in what you're doing is to do it well.

Let's begin with a personal example: Many years ago, I hated mowing my lawn. There were several reasons. First, there was a steep hill in my back yard with a fence at the bottom that made it very difficult to mow. Second, there were no exterior outlets on the front of my house, so I had to use a series of extension cords to bring power to the front yard for the electric weed eater. The cords were just short enough that there was a corner I couldn't trim properly. It would have been unsafe to add another cord to the chain, and so that corner went untrimmed.

Week after week, I'd go outside, annoyed before I even picked up a tool. I'd do the bare minimum passable job, skip the corner I couldn't reach, and put the grass-covered tools back.

One day, I decided to start approaching it differently. I had to get it done—there was no way around it other than hiring someone, and I didn't have the money at the time—and having a bad attitude was getting me nowhere. I tried to enjoy mowing, and challenged myself to do a great job, taking pride in it and finding peace in trying to achieve perfection.

I practiced allowing myself to exist in the moment instead of focusing on what I'd rather be doing or what I had to do next. The quality of my work increased measurably and I discovered that doing a poor job had only been saving about ten minutes.

Think about how this idea applies to your own life. Drafting an email or fixing a broken railing in your home, putting your child to bed or wrapping holiday presents. Cleaning. Organizing. Preparing a meal. Taking time to do things *well* instead of racing to get them done and out of the way improves safety and quality. Just as importantly, you'll feel better. As someone who was always disorganized, I never would have guessed that I would take pride in organizing the glove box of my car. As someone who was always in a rush, I never thought I'd enjoy taking the time to measure the distance between picture frames to line them up perfectly on a wall. I've known many people who have adopted this mentality, but most didn't do it until their twilight years. Do it now and enjoy the benefits forever. Engage with the present.

Practical mindfulness may be difficult to adopt, but by training yourself to **Check In**, etc., you're already practicing this in some ways. You're paying attention to the moment in a way that you haven't in the past. The only thing left is to slow down and try to enjoy everything you do. This type of mentality change will quickly become apparent to others; if you reject the urge to "half-ass" things, you will shed any reputation you may have cultivated as someone who "half-asses" things.

To practice this, take a task you dislike doing—chores are usually good for this—and implement these strategies and principles. At first, don't try to force yourself to enjoy the task, but rather try to *enjoy the challenge inherent in doing it well.* Stop your mind from wandering to your next responsibility or the other chores you need to do or the fun things that you could be doing. Be in the moment, relax, and commit to doing a good job. You'll be amazed at how much this simple strategy improves your overall quality of life.

Quick Review

Practical mindfulness means focusing on what you're doing, performing to the best of your ability, and resisting the urge to think about what you could/should be doing otherwise or what you have to do afterward. This will cause you to enjoy the task more; increase the safety, precision, and efficiency of your work; and improve the quality of your output.

Glossary

Action Question   A specific question you train yourself to ask every time you find yourself in a certain type of situation.

Arrival Check-In   A predefined **Check-In** that is referenced upon arriving at a new setting or situation.

Batch / Batching   See **Task Batching**.

Big Batching Day   A day on which you perform tasks that should recur on a monthly basis (or somewhat close to monthly basis).

Blocker   In a **Serial** relationship, the necessary step that is interrupted by one or more **Dependents**. **Serializing** is performed by attaching **Dependents** to **Blockers**.

Check-In / Checking In   A tool for drastically increasing awareness that consists of habitually asking a series of **Action Questions** before and after every single thing you do.

Departure Check-In   A predefined **Check-In** that's referenced before leaving a setting or situation.

Dependent   In a **Serial** relationship, a task you'd like to remember that is attached to a **Blocker**, or a task that *must* be performed.

Front-Load /   See **Task Front-Loading**.
Front-Loading

Moment of   The moment in which you decided to perform an
Intention   action or task.

Peripheral   Work you need to do in order to complete a
Workload   **Primary Workload**, but otherwise wouldn't do.

Primary   The main purpose of a task.
Workload

Redundancy   Ensuring that you're doing an adequate job of
                          Checking In by exposing each transition (the trip
                          from one location to the next) to two
                          independent reviews.

Serialize /   See **Task Serialization**.
Serialization /
Serial
Relationship

Situational   A concept taught at all levels of emergency
Awareness   response and law enforcement that involves
                          developing a heightened awareness of your
                          surroundings in order to identify potential
                          threats.

Task Batching   Performing several related tasks together;
                          organizing tasks so as to minimize the total time,
                          resources, or risk required to perform them.

Task Front-Loading	The act of getting tasks out of the way as soon as possible, within reason. Summarized with the slogan, "Do a favor for 'future you.'"
Task Serialization	Ordering tasks such that you essentially *have* to perform one in order to perform another.

9780692425695